M̶E̶E̶T̶I̶N̶G
THE
WORLD
Ministering Cross-Culturally

Published by:
New Hope
P.O. Box 12065
Birmingham, Alabama 35202-2065

Cover design and illustration by Barry Graham

Dewey Decimal Classification: 261.2
Subject Headings: CHRISTIANITY AND OTHER RELIGIONS
                           CROSS CULTURAL STUDIES
                           ETHNOPSYCHOLOGY
                           WITNESSING

ISBN 1-56309-020-1
N924105•5M•0692

Contents

◆

Cross-cultural Communication and Witness

Mark Snowden

Digging into Their Culture

This planet has more than 5 billion people, but the real world for most of us is much smaller. Unless you travel over a large territory, your world is probably the small society or culture where you live each day. Effective communication serves us with a means of adapting to our family, co-workers, and friends. Communication helps us to define another person's viewpoint and compare that with our own. We all need to feel free to communicate with others.

One of the greatest obstacles to genuine communication occurs when we forget that when we communicate events, we also communicate from our own experiences—which can be very personal. Spiritual experiences, learning experiences, human relation experiences, and phenomenal experiences, when communicated, are all subject to interpretation based on our personality and our own culture. People who study such things say we are unable to communicate an experience without inserting our own personal bias.

Because we are all blessed by intellect, our "hearing" is based on how we respond to the experience emotionally and mentally. When another individual receives our message, he or she will go through a similar filtering process.

Our communication will carry with it an accumulation of our personality, which will be greatly influenced by our culture. People from other countries rarely communicate without risking an interpretation from the point of view of their respective cultures.

REMEMBER: To effectively communicate with someone from another country, start by examining *your* personal background, life-style, and life experiences.

When we communicate our experiences, we can be selective in terms of what we have experienced and how we want it to be interpreted by others. Personality and culture intervene to influence us to see and hear as we might be accustomed rather than to see and hear the actual truth of the experience. Most Americans are very selective in relation to what we see, and even more selective in how we will communicate the experience that has been witnessed.

How do we communicate best? If we are to communicate, then we must abandon the desire to have others respond to an experience as we have. Instead, the communication goal is to have others experience an event in their own way, and rejoice in mutual acceptance of the fact that the event indeed did occur.

When a person becomes poised to communicate an experience with another, there is an internal process that occurs. Before speaking you rapidly think, How can I say this? We are motivated to communicate our Christian experience with the hope that it will be understood by the person. The Holy Spirit does help us in our communications efforts! You can always rely on that, so let's take a look at how God can help us be more useful in witnessing.

You rack your brain and prayerfully search for the right words that best tell your experience. Then you try several combinations of words, gestures, and images. You actually try to paint a mental picture of the experience. And then, humph, they just don't understand. Imagine!

If the person you are trying to talk to cannot relate to any of your messages and possibly misunderstands, you might become frustrated. But don't give up! You have taken a great first step toward communication.

REMEMBER: It is important to understand symbols (images and messages) that are most familiar to the one with whom you are communicating.

Another person's culture has strongly influenced their politics, economics, and sensitivity toward race and religion; understand your attempts at communication can never be easily separated from the culture of the person on the receiving end. The words, hand gestures, and ideas you use must be meaningful to you and *especially* to them; otherwise, misunderstandings will pop up.

Even though you may have something in common with a person from another social environment (same job, possibly similar ethnic origin, kids going to the same school, living just next door, etc.), the clash most often comes with the *values and norms* of the separate cultures from which both of you have been so emotionally, but separately, involved. If you don't catch this early on, either of you might feel threatened—even afraid. One or both of you will probably end up feeling left out or uncomfortable in the presence of the other. We all cling to our roots! While your brain may be telling you (with unholy pride) that this situation appears to be very reasonable, the tuggings of your heart will possibly cause problems for both parties involved.

The saying that "the ground is level at the foot of the cross" is important here. Rather than placing yourself in jeopardy by ignoring the unfamiliar hills and valleys of another's value system, try to position your communication on levels that you both understand.

Understanding Culture
You don't have to be an international expert to understand all the quirks or ideals of another person's background. An understanding of culture in general will help you, though, be more sensitive to the needs of others.

Culture is the sum total of the way people live. Individuals really develop a culture unto themselves, since no two individuals (even couples married 50 years!) ever live *exactly* alike. When all these individuals live together within a similar environment, culture begins to grow as the larger group experiences common sequences of activities.

What about the person from another culture that you have met? It is possible that that person's family has even developed their own private culture. Maybe you find that your family is unique. We all fit within several cultures:

9

Community cultures	City cultures
Urban neighborhood cultures	Provincial cultures
State cultures	National cultures
Multinational cultures	Continental cultures

We could even say there is a world culture! There is a world culture in the sense that there are areas of experience that have enough similarity to make it possible to communicate across cultural lines to all areas of the world. In the era of faster travel, technological advances in telecommunications, and information access, Marshall McLuhan's term *global village* certainly begins to apply.

As you prepare sociological or cultural ideas, keep in mind that the more insulated the person is from your culture, the more alien any new idea will appear to him.

Did you know there are cultures where a decision is *never* made by an individual, but rather, it is made by the group, or at least receives approval by the group?

REMEMBER: Individuals and groups, as well as nations, try desperately to preserve values and convictions which they have long maintained and consider precious.

Communication Channels

Most readers will be seeking personal ways to communicate with a new international friend. You might just be considering talking or writing a letter. However, there are several channels to consider communicating with individuals both in a mass-appeal and personal way.

Media influences cross-cultural communications efforts. You or your church can use radio, television, film, newspapers, magazines, etc., to reach an audience of many from the same cultural background. Mass media can:(1) reach a large audience rapidly; (2) communicate knowledge and spread information; (3) lead to changes in weakly held attitudes.

However, the formation and change of strongly held attitudes is best accomplished by interpersonal channels.

Interpersonal channels are those that involve a face-to-face exchange between two or more people. These channels have greater effectiveness in the face of resistance or apathy.

Interpersonal communication can benefit by a supportive use of media such as print and group or individual electronic media such as audio- or videocassettes, films, books, tracts, and possibly other media. Interpersonal channels can: (1) allow a two-way exchange of ideas. Questions that arise can be answered immediately. (2) persuade receiving individuals to form or change strongly held attitudes.

REMEMBER: Personal communication comes to mind first, but mass communication is also an effective tool.

Levels of Communication
The most helpful key to good communication with those of another culture is to be aware that communication takes place at three progressive levels.

The first level is communication between a person who comes from one field of experience and who is looking for a way to communicate meaningfully with a person from another field of experience. This might be you or it might be the other person or group as well. Cooperatively searching out common ground will be easier in this level, but potentially more likely to contain misunderstandings. The more information you can access, the better your attempts at communication will be. (This is why companies and governments put such a high price on information gathering.) Here are five categories to investigate:

1. Physical: Hunger, desires, sexual attitudes
2. Self-preservation: Protection from unknown danger
3. Sociological: Love, affection, belonging
4. Self-appreciation: Self-esteem, self-respect, and respect for others
5. Fulfillment: Achievement of goals one is capable of attaining, perceived potential

WARNING: Double-check the accuracy of your sources—including your own personal experiences!

The second level of communication can be considered subcultures of a greater culture related to the first level. These subcultures, then, are more personal, but not as personal as we might be inclined to think. But neither should they constitute barriers in communication. At this level of communication, we find certain characteristics, such as:

1. *Better understanding of the jargon.* We must be cautious not to assume that non-Christians in *any* culture are totally familiar with the jargon Christians use.

2. *Acceptance of the content to be presented.* There might not be widespread opposition due to prejudice, or a clash with the value system in your area. If everyone is in agreement with the content being presented, we naturally approach it differently. If we can get to this point, then we can deal with needs that are not as superficial as those back in the first level of communication. We dig deeper into a person's personality, needs, and spiritual perspective. This will help you deal more with causes than with symptoms.

3. *Existence of areas of common interest.* The person or whole group might not be in total agreement concerning the direction that should be taken, but they can be generally concerned about the fact that problems do exist and that they must be solved. Again, this puts tremendous importance on investigation before communication.

The third level of communication is reached when those communicating are prepared to share very intimately. At this level, you both will be able to share details of your personalities, which both would otherwise reveal only to very close family members or to intimate friends.

Ring That Doorbell!

Unselfishly caring for the eternal welfare of a lost person is the mandate of Christ. Contemporary Christian music singer Chuck Girrard wrote a song telling his experience of witness, witness, witness without results until he realized that he had given out tracts and not love.

Christ can best be revealed to others in self-examination of motives, investigation into the other's culture, and overcoming barriers through a closer relationship.

This is not a license to procrastinate, nor is it encouraging just jumping in without much thought. Through prayer, Bible study, and identification of common values, a witness can be effectively communicated.

◆

Meeting the Hispanic World

Daniel Sanchez

The need to have ministries among Hispanic Americans is supported by the fact that they now number more than 20 million and are projected to become the largest minority group in this country within the next decade.[1] There is quite a bit of diversity within this group composed of Mexican Americans, Puerto Rican Americans, Cuban Americans, Central and South Americans, Spaniards, and others from Spanish-speaking areas. At the same time, the various subgroups have many things in common, the greatest of which is the Spanish culture and language.

To be effective in meeting and ministering to Hispanic Americans, we must be informed about the ways in which they are different as well as the ways they are alike. With this in mind, let's focus first on the major subgroups which make up the Hispanic American population in this country. Then we will give our attention to what they have in common. In the last section we will make some suggestions about how to minister to them intelligently and effectively.

Hispanic People in the United States
Let's look at the major groups which make up the Hispanic population.[2] I will begin with Mexican Americans, who have the distinction of being the largest group among Hispanics (63 percent),[3] and of having been in this country the longest. Because they are native to the Southwest, their ancestors were there before this area became a part of the United States. Due to continued immigration, some Mexican Americans have arrived in the US in more recent years and even weeks. There are, therefore, varying degrees of adaptation to the predominant culture in this country.

Some are very fluent in English while others can hardly understand it. While Mexican Americans are concentrated in the southwestern part of the US, significant numbers of them are found in the Great Lake states and other industrial areas.[4]

Puerto Rican Americans constitute the second largest group among Hispanics, comprising 12 percent of their population. They have been US citizens since 1917 and can therefore travel freely between the island and the mainland.[5] Puerto Ricans living in the mainland are concentrated in the Northeast (54 percent live in New York City). Chicago has the second largest Puerto Rican population, followed by other cities with smaller settlements. As they adjust to life in the mainland, they have to deal with differences in culture, language, and climate. Like Mexican Americans, Puerto Ricans have been a part of the US for several generations and have made varying degrees of adaptation to the predominant culture of this country.[6]

The third Hispanic group in terms of length of residence, though not the third in terms of population (5 percent), is Cuban Americans. Although some Cubans had resided in the US since the mid-1800s, more than 650,000 attained political refuge in the United States after the 1959 revolution. Their entry was made easier by several factors: (1) the US hostility toward Cuba; (2) a desire on the part of many Americans to help them adjust to this country; (3) the fact that a large number of those who came were well-educated professionals.[7] The Cuban American population increased through the second wave of immigration which came by way of the Mariel Boat Lift. Cubans are primarily concentrated in large metropolitan areas such as Miami, New York City, Jersey City, Los Angeles, and Chicago. One of the distinguishing marks of Cuban Americans is that they have a disproportionately large number of elderly people.[8]

Central and South Americans constitute the third largest Hispanic group (11 percent) in this country.[9] Because they come from 18 different countries and speak other languages in addition to Spanish, they cannot be viewed as a homogeneous group. "They represent differing social strata, regional attachments, and ethnocultural backgrounds."[10] Attracted by the possibility of political stability, economic improvement, and educational opportunities, an unprecedented number of Central and South Americans have come to the US in recent years. Once here they move toward the large metropolitan areas with specific groups concentrating in certain cities (e.g., Guatemalans favor Los Angeles, Hondurans flock to the Gulf Coast). Because the highly trained and skilled have had the resources to come to this country, many immigrants from Central and South America are middle-class.[11]

As you can see from the discussion above, there are many differences between the various Hispanic American groups. Despite their many differences they do have many things in common. One of these commonalities is the high value they place on the family. For a significant number of Hispanic Americans the family is the center of their social life. This includes not only the nuclear family (mother, father, and the children) but the extended family (including grandparents, aunts, cousins, in-laws, etc.).

A second thing which Hispanic Americans have in common relates to their religious tradition. Even though the majority of them are nominal Roman Catholics, many of them believe that their cultural identity is closely related to their religious tradition. In other words, they believe that "to be Hispanic is to be Roman Catholic."

A third commonality is that they are experiencing cultural and socioeconomic transition brought about by the fact that they relate to two cultures. On the one hand, they have the desire and the need to retain their culture, while on the other hand, they are motivated by the educational system, the news media, and peer groups to adopt the language and customs of Anglo society. Because of the varying responses to this transition, there are those who speak no English at all, those who speak no Spanish at all, and those who are bilingual.[12] Adaptation to the culture also creates tensions among Hispanic Americans. The second dimension of this transition (socioeconomic) is due to a large extent to the fact that Hispanic Americans have moved rapidly from a rural life-style to one which is mostly metropolitan. Two contributing factors to this have been the change in occupation of the permanent residents (from agricultural to clerical and professional) and the immigration of skilled and semi-skilled persons. While these cultural and socioeconomic transitions have represented new opportunities for Hispanic Americans, they have also created a great deal of tension in their families and have often undermined the harmony and unity they have longed for.

A fourth thing which many Hispanic Americans have in common is the need for higher educational attainment. While some segments of the Hispanic population have made remarkable progress in this area,[13] regrettably other segments are lagging far behind.[14] This helps to create a cycle of poverty which is often passed from one generation to another.

Hispanic Americans also share the desire to celebrate. Even though many of the families live below the poverty line and face many hardships, they look forward to the days when they can put all their troubles behind (even for a moment) and celebrate the joyous experiences of life such as births, birthdays, anniversaries, religious days, and national holidays. This provides an opportunity for them to fellowship with their group and to affirm the values they have in common.

Do's and Don'ts of Ministry
How can we minister to them in the name of our Lord and Saviour Jesus Christ? We will answer this question by first discussing a series of don'ts and then a series of do's.

The series of don'ts is as follows:

1. Don't stereotype them. In other words, don't lump them all into one category. For example, all Hispanic Americans are not newly arrived immigrants; some have been here for several generations. All of them are not migrant workers; some are highly trained professionals. On the other hand, all Hispanic Americans are not wealthy; there are many who live below the poverty line. In order to relate to them in a redemptive manner, therefore, make an effort to know their particular group and individuals within the group.

16

2. Don't treat them in a paternalistic manner. In other words, in trying to help them don't do everything for them. Don't do all the planning for them. Don't try to make all the decisions for them. If they are in need, it is better to help them in such a way that they can assume responsibility for themselves. Enable them to help themselves.

3. Don't discuss religion. Due to the fact that many of them believe their identity is tied in with their religion, it is better not to get into a discussion about religion. What you can and should do is discuss *relationship*. In other words, stress their relationship with Jesus Christ. After cultivating a friendship, share the plan of salvation with them. Once they get to know Jesus Christ, they will often begin to examine their relationship with their church. If the first thing they hear from you, however, is "you ought to leave your church and join mine," they will be completely turned-off. So stress *relationship* not *religion*.

With these don'ts in mind let's turn to some do's.

1. Because of the deep concern that many Hispanic Americans have about their families, do be involved in ministries which relate to this concern. Some of the traditional approaches to children (Vacation Bible School, Backyard Bible Clubs, day camp) can still be *very effective*. In addition to these, activities such as marriage enrichment workshops (or retreats), ministries to single mothers, home Bible studies focusing on the family, meals and social activities for the elderly, and Bible studies for young women can be of tremendous help to Hispanic American families.

2. Because of the religious traditions of many Hispanic Americans, often nurturing activities such as the ones just mentioned are needed before they will be willing to hear the gospel. It is encouraging to know that unprecedented numbers of Hispanics are responding to the gospel.[15]

3. Because of the cultural transitions which many Hispanic Americans are experiencing, do be involved in ministries which help them to deal with these tensions. Some of these activities are: English-as-a-second-language classes, citizenship classes, classes about the Anglo-American culture (especially for new arrivals). To address socioeconomic transition, offer classes in such areas as typ-

ing, sewing, computer skills, and income-tax preparation.

4. To address educational concerns do activities such as individual tutoring, leading classes at church to help children with their homework, adopting a local public school, and being available to help the teachers with those students who are lagging behind.

5. Because of the desire of Hispanic Americans to celebrate, having fellowships at church in honor of birthdays, anniversaries, and holidays can provide a place for them to meet one another as well as those in the church who are interested in ministering to them. Dramas at Easter and Christmas can have a special appeal to them.

God has brought a missions field to our doorsteps; let us respond by meeting them and ministering to them in the name of our Lord Jesus Christ.

◆

Meeting the Chinese World

C. Thomas Wright

I was the only Anglo at the head table of a Chinese banquet. The magnificent roast pig was placed in front of us. The host removed the pig's ear with his chopsticks and placed it on my bowl of rice. He was honoring his guest. His guest was horrified. My chopsticks trembled as they directed the ear toward my mouth. The Anglo culture within screamed "No!" The Chinese observers nodded and murmured with approval as I consumed the ear. The Anglo culture had met Chinese culture. Neither culture is better or worse. They are just different. It is important for us to learn the differences and similarities in each other's culture, particularly if we want to earn credibility for friendship and witness.

Meeting the Chinese world means meeting nearly a quarter of the world's population, a population that includes one of the largest ethnic groups in the United States. So you are very likely to meet people of Chinese ancestry. This chapter introduces you to the history, culture, and religion of the Chinese people. It also offers some practical tips on sharing the gospel of Jesus Christ with Chinese people.

Chinese People in the United States
The Chinese are but one of the many immigrant and refugee groups in the United States. The original population of North America was native American (American Indian). They were joined by immigrants from Central America, Europe, and Asia. Chinese tradesmen were in North America as early as 1517. It was the European immigrants, however, that quickly outnumbered other groups. Eventually these European immigrants began to call them-

selves Americans to the exclusion of the other immigrants. But the United States had become a stew pot of refugees and immigrants. And no one of those immigrant groups was any more American than the others. The melting pot of different cultures refused to melt. Every refugee and immigrant culture remained intact to some degree. Even the European "hidden ethnics," like Scots and Germans, have maintained their heart culture. The Scots may not be physically different enough from other Anglos to pick out of a crowd but they have maintained cultural ties to the homeland.

Chinese in the United States are immigrants, students, or visitors. There is a difference between immigrants and refugees. Refugees are forced to leave their country due to political or personal danger. Refugee groups in the United States include Cubans, Vietnamese, Eastern Europeans, Ethiopians, and Nicaraguans. Immigrants choose to leave their country to pursue a better life-style. Immigrants include Asian Indians, most Europeans, Koreans, and Chinese. The Chinese in the US are considered immigrants even though many came here fleeing political unrest.

Christians should consider the potential influence of a Chinese student or visitor that returns to China with a newfound faith in Jesus Christ. That is particularly important since missionaries are not allowed in the country. The Chinese population in the United States has grown from 758 Chinese residents in 1850 to 1,645,472 Chinese registered in the 1990 census. Chinese immigrants initially were drawn to what they called the Golden Mountain during the California gold rush. Other Chinese came to work on the western expansion of the railroads. Still others came to escape civil war, natural disasters, or Communism. The first immigrants soon began to bring in family and clan members. Chinese researcher Betty Lee Sung has identified a major reason for immigration.

"One of the most important reasons why the parents immigrated to the United States was for the sake of the children. They came to open up a brighter future for their progeny."[1] Prejudice and cultural differences caused many Chinese immigrants to create and live in Chinatowns.

Chinese immigrants are not limited to laborers called bitter strength or coolies. In 1980, more than half of the US Asian population held professional, technical, or administrative occupations.[2] These Chinese are well-educated people with a good command of the English language.

Expect a dramatic increase in the stateside Chinese population as 1997 approaches. At that time Hong Kong comes under control of the People's Republic of China, having been a British Crown colony since 1841. Emigration out of Hong Kong has grown from 20,000 per year in the early eighties to 100,000 a year in 1989 and 1990. Many leading businesses are also setting up legal headquarters in other countries.[3]

Chinese Culture

Our family had gone to the Asian market to get some rice. An older woman was wearing pink fluffy slippers as she collected her groceries. There was nothing wrong with wearing pink fluffy slippers to the store. They were warm and comfortable. However, our western culture says, "Pink fluffy slippers are for the home." Culture defines how and why we act the way we act. It also defines how we look at events and how we respond to those events. Culture includes our preferences for food, music, language, clothing, family, art, values, and religion. Western culture approves the use of forks. Asian culture prefers chopsticks. Neither culture is wrong, but each is different.

The Chinese culture is the oldest continuous civilization on earth. Their languages predate English by thousands of years. From A.D. 1150 the Chinese called themselves the Middle Kingdom. They believed China was the geographic center of civilization. Anglo maps of today reflect our similar bias toward western civilization. A new map, called the Peters Projection map, has recently become available that accurately shows the proportion of land mass from East and West. It looks strange to us because we are accustomed to maps focused on North America.[4]

When meeting the Chinese world, it is important to distinguish between the culture of the American Born Chinese (ABC) and Overseas Born Chinese (OBC). In 1980, more than 46 percent of the Chinese population was born in the United States. The ABC experience often is similar to that of Steven A. Chin, a staff reporter for the *San Francisco Examiner*. He writes about the racial stereotypes and prejudice directed toward him. "No, I'm not related to Bruce Lee or Charlie Chan. Naturally, I speak English well. I was born and raised here. I'm from New York City—honest." He continues, "I was a new breed—American in my ways, Asian in appearance, but essentially void of Chinese culture. Chinese call us 'juk sing' or hollow bamboo."[5]

Many ABCs are proud of their Asian heritage but are culturally and linguistically North American. ABCs often respond well to English speaking Chinese-culture congregations. OBCs respond better to Chinese-culture congregations that use the heart language. The heart language is the language in which a person was raised. Many people who are fluent in a second language continue to prefer the heart language for important business and personal matters.

Language is an important part of any culture. Language includes spoken words and unspoken actions. A familiar Chinese action is that Chinese greet each other with a slight bow. The hands are clasped at chest level. However, many Chinese have adapted the western style of greeting with a handshake. Many western actions and mannerisms are seen by Chinese to be impolite. Western familiarity with leaders and older peers is often seen as disrespectful. Respect of elders is very important to the Chinese.

The two major spoken Chinese languages are Mandarin and Cantonese. But there are many other Chinese dialects that are important heart languages. The Soochow or Hakka languages, for example, are widespread but completely different from Mandarin or Cantonese. Chinese languages are tonal. That means the word *Ma* can mean *mother*, *horse*, or *plant* depending on the tone. Chinese characters, however, are the same in each language. That is helpful when giving someone Chinese Bibles, tracts, or other materials. Bible studies or worship should be conducted in the heart language.

The OBCs have different needs depending on how long they have been in the United States. Do not assume that any immigrants and refugees will assimilate (accept) the new culture. For example, the United States Embassy in Bangkok sponsored a yearly fourth of July party. US citizens who had been in Bangkok for 30 years attended. These Anglos and their children still spoke English, liked hamburgers, and used a fork to eat. Chinese who have been in the US for 30 years likewise have maintained their heart language and culture.

Chinese sociologist Fei Tasio Tung has an interesting analogy of the differences between Chinese and Anglo cultures. He compares western society to "a bunch of hay tied together by a rope. The rope represents the law and the constitution. All [people] are equal under the law." The Chinese society, however, is more like a "stone thrown into the water creating ripples. If the stone is a small one, there are less ripples. . . . The stone is the head of the family. The ripples are the descendants."[6] The stone should receive greater respect than the ripples.

Cultural differences also include the western nuclear family versus the Chinese extended family, western self-confidence versus Chinese humility, western impatience versus Chinese patience, and western confrontation versus Chinese conciliation.

It also is important to understand the differences between the democratic Republic of China on Taiwan and the Communist People's Republic of China on the mainland. The democratic Nationalist Chinese government fled to Taiwan in 1949 when the Communist party overthrew China. The Nationalistic Chinese on Taiwan consider themselves the true Chinese government in exile. Taiwan maintains use of the Chinese flag adopted at the collapse of the Manchu dynasty in 1911. Mainland China uses the Communist flag adopted in 1949.

Chinese Religion

As many as 95 percent of the Chinese people practice a mixture of folk religion, Taoism, Confucianism, and Buddhism. Taoism (pronounced dah-o-ism) emphasizes the union (harmony) of humankind and nature. This perspective often is seen in Chinese art. A typical painting will show tall mountains and broad rivers with a small fisherman in his boat. It is also within Taoism that the familiar yin-yang circle functions, supposedly, to bring inner peace. The common dragon symbol represents the yin (cold, moist, passive, dark, feminine); the tiger symbol represents the yang (hot, dry, active, light, male). Christians know that inner peace is reached only through a relationship with Jesus Christ.

The second part of the Chinese religious mixture is Confucianism. Confucianism is more an ethical system than a religion. Bette Bao Lord, wife of the former US Ambassador to China, describes Confucianism: "To Confucius . . . proper conduct . . . was the measure of a man. To ask mere mortals to discipline their thoughts as well as their actions would be asking too much—form would suffice. And so the Chinese embraced ritual, the ultimate form."[7] Confucius (B.C. 551-446) developed rules to govern basic human relationships. The central Confucian virtue of family results in ancestor worship. In the United States ancestor worship perhaps is called more accurately ancestor practices. Many stateside Chinese perform the ancestor practices out of respect and cultural identity, not out of religious worship. Confucius taught that humankind is basically good, so there is no divine punishment or reward.

Taoist and Confucian beliefs blended with Buddhism after the first century B.C. Like other world religions, Buddhism teaches salvation by works. Buddhism encourages believers to do good things. The believer will be rewarded if lifetime good outweighs bad. Many people interpret that to mean: be good 51 percent of the time and do whatever you want the remaining time. Chinese religion adopted the Buddhist design for ornate temples and embraced Buddhist compassion through orphanages and hospitals.

Christianity arrived in China more than 1,500 years ago. Growth was slow and difficult. There were still fewer than one million Christians in China at the beginning of this century. It is estimated the number of Christians in China grew from 1 million in 1946 to more than 50 million in 1986. Christians suffered severe persecution during that 40 years. They were imprisoned, tortured, and humiliated. During the latter part of the Cultural Revolution it was illegal to hold Christian meetings. Sharon E. Mumper, editor at large for *Evangelical Missions Quarterly*, says, "Part of the foundation for growth was laid by the very Cultural Revolution that sought to destroy the church and other social institutions.... When the chaos ended, an entire generation was completely disillusioned with Communism and ready for something—anything—that offered hope."[8] The Cultural Revolution began in 1966 as an attempt to purge "revisionist thought." Christianity, education, and social reforms were all considered revisionist thought. Thousands of students were formed into the Red Guard to enforce the purge. The Cultural Revolution ended in 1976 with the death of Mao Zedong and the arrest of his supporters, often called the "Gang of Four." The Chinese consider that period "the 10 lost years."[9] It was a decade of horror and repression. But like the bamboo, the Chinese bent with the wind, but returned upright when the wind had past.

Recent Chinese immigrants may respond to Christianity in terms of the negative stories told by the Communists. Communist leaders tied Christianity to imperialism and cultural invasion by the West. Some young Chinese are surprised to find the number of people in the United States that profess Christianity. Communist propaganda had led them to believe that no intelligent people still practiced religion.

Building Cross-Cultural Friendships

Jesus is our best example of how to make friends across cultures. Jesus was communicating across cultures when He met the woman at the well in John 4:7-42. The first thing Jesus did was to take the initiative to make a friend. She was a Samaritan and a woman. Jesus did not let cultural or racial prejudice interfere with His outreach. He knew all people need salvation from sin.

Then He began to earn credibility with the woman. He found out about her needs and her family. He clearly and accurately shared with her the gospel of the Messiah. He showed her that a relationship with God in Jesus Christ was different from any other world religion. He encouraged her to use her influence in the community. She in turn brought many other Samaritans to meet Jesus. He built relationships with them too. Many Samaritans became believers from that first contact.

Other examples of His cross-cultural ministry include the gentile centurion in Matthew 8:5-13 and the Canaanite woman in Matthew 15:21-28. The Great Commission of Matthew 28:19-20 particularly teaches the importance of every Christian sharing the gospel with every person on earth. The Greek word for "all nations" in those verses shows there should be no cultural or racial preference.

Follow the example of Jesus to meet the Chinese world. Take the initiative to make a friend. Find out about them. What is their heart language? Are they ABC or OBC? How long have they been here? Give them a Bible and other Christian materials in their heart language.

Carefully share that Christianity is different from all other world religions. Help the Chinese person understand the life, teachings, atoning death, and resurrection of Jesus. Do not attack the old religions. Focus on introducing the person to Jesus.

Many people incorrectly define religion as a system to make people good. In that definition, if all religions teach people to be good then all religions are of equal value. But the Bible teaches that being good is not enough to reach heaven. Christianity teaches there is a difference in being holy and in being good. The only way to be holy is for a person to ask the Holy Spirit of God to come live inside of him or her. Then good actions are a result of holiness in a transformed heart and mind. A person asks the Holy Spirit to live inside of him or her through a relationship with Jesus Christ. Jesus is the unique Son of God who died for all humankind and paid for our sin. Sin is best defined as disobeying God. Every person has disobeyed God and needs forgiveness for that sin. Jesus Christ is the only way to receive forgiveness of sin, be filled with the Holy Spirit, and go to heaven. This explanation is helpful to those in a salvation by works religion.

Every culture prefers to worship in its heart language. Help Chinese people to find a worship service that reflects his or her language and culture.

◆

Meeting the Hindu World

Norma Charles

Hinduism, one of the oldest and most complex religions in the world, dates back almost 3,000 years. Archaeological discoveries illustrate that over time it incorporated religious practices of different groups. Aryans, who invaded India around 1500 B.C., held certain plants and animals sacred, parallels to which are seen in Hinduism as practiced today. Nevertheless, Hinduism is unique; it has no organized church, no single recognized leader, and no scriptural authority. Today, 82 percent of Asian Indians are its adherents. That equals 600 million people, including 2 to 3 million in the United States.

Following is a brief description on basic beliefs of the Hindus, their cultural background, and the ways of witnessing and communicating the gospel to them.

Basic Beliefs of the Hindus
BRAHMAN (God). The fundamental belief is in one imminent, all-inclusive, impersonal, and unknowable spiritual reality, called Brahman. Hindus worship other gods as well. According to Hindu scriptures, there are 330 million gods to choose from as individual and family gods. But the belief is that all gods are aspects or manifestations of the one main god, Brahman. Brahman is the universal spirit and is personalized as Brahma the Creator, Vishnu the Preserver, and Shiva the Destroyer. Hindus also believe in incarnations and worship two of Vishnu's ten mythical incarnations: Rama and Krishna. Belief in demons, spirits, magic, astrology, and superstitions, is also common.
MAN. Man is not inherently or permanently worthful. Man is part of God. Man is not a sinner. Atma, or the eternal soul

of man, is a spark of divinity in man but we do not know it because of ignorance. Maya, the illusionary world, keeps us from understanding this identity but one can realize one's union or oneness with Brahman.

The goal of life is to find out who you are and to live that way and to pass beyond illusion to become one with Brahman. To achieve this goal, a Hindu can renounce this world and go through any trouble.

KARMA (actions). Karma means actions. A Hindu believes that his present life is determined by his action in the past and his future life will be determined by his actions today. The law of *Karma* (the law of deeds) is inescapable—good actions bring rewards and bad actions punishment. You can be born in a higher form of life or a lower form of life. By performing righteous acts one can move towards liberation from the cycle of endless births, but by one's evil acts one will move further away from it.

MOKSHA (Salvation). The Hindu's hope is the realization of their true identity with the supreme soul, to be absorbed into Brahman. The goal of life is to achieve liberation from the cycle of rebirths, samsara (worldly life) or transmigration of soul (reincarnation caused by Karma) and finally attain Moksha (eternal bliss). Moksha means complete release from the wheel of samsara and from Karma itself. There are three ways for a Hindu to achieve salvation: through knowledge (Gnana yoga), through devotion (Bhakti yoga), and through works (Karma yoga).

CREATION. Creation is a temporary worthless illusion (Maya). Brahman caused the illusion of creation. There is no beginning or conclusion, only endless cycles of creation and destruction.

SIN. Hindus do not have the concept of sin in the sense of guilt or rebellion against God or in the sense of broken relationship with God. Man makes mistakes because of ignorance (*avidya*).

CASTE SYSTEM. The caste system is a unique feature of Hindu religion. There are four main castes: Brahmins (priests), Kshatriyas (warriors), Vaisyas (businessmen, professionals, and traders), and Sudras (artisans and laborers). Caste rules prevent Hindus from eating, marrying, and mixing with the people of the other castes.

WORSHIP. Most Hindus worship daily. Their worship is not congregational but individualistic. Many Hindu homes have a family shrine room or a corner in a room with idols. Their worship is recitation of scriptures, chanting prayers, singing bhajans, offering flowers and sweets, burning incense before the idols, and fasting.

HINDU SCRIPTURES. Hindu scriptures are the *Vedas*, the *Upanishads*, the two epics the *Ramayana* and the *Mahabharata*, the *Puranas*, and the *Bhagavad Gita*.

CULTURAL BACKGROUND OF THE HINDUS. The majority of Hindus are Asian Indians. Asian Indians are very friendly and hospitable people. They respect their guests and visitors. Asian Indians usually offer their visitors something to eat or drink.

Asian Indians are basically event oriented people but their sense of time is based on the importance of the person or event. Asian Indians like to invite their friends in their homes and they like to be invited too. You need to know that most Hindus do not eat meat or egg and none eat beef.

Most Asian Indians can speak two to three native languages including English. They like to talk about their family, culture, customs, and food. Americans are treated as important persons.

Asian Indian women have special respect and place in the house, but widows do not have much respect in Hinduism. The constitution of India gives equal rights to women and men. Marriage is a religious necessity and marriages are arranged. Dating, divorce, and remarriages are socially unacceptable.

Indian Hindus live in extended family units with the relatives of the father under the authority of the oldest male person and elders. Hindus look upon children as gifts from the gods. The son is still a religious necessity.

Hindus usually take off their shoes before entering a temple, mosque, kitchen, or going near a tomb. Cows are sacred Hindu symbols. Hindus believe music is divine in its origin and its ultimate function is to help them realize God.

Asian Indians take care of their elderly. Their family devotion and affection is outstanding. Asian Indians are very religious people and very tradition bound.

Hindrances to Hindu Conversion
•Old religious traditions and deep rooted customs, of which a Hindu is so much a part. Conversion is seen as a threat to the extended family unit as well as a disgrace to family traditions.
•Hindus think Christianity is a religion of the white people (west) and in India, a religion of the poor (low caste). Therefore, Christianity is inferior to Hinduism in many ways. Conversion means change.
•Nominal Christians, their habits, life-style, and superficial practice of Christianity is another main hindrance.
•Hindus believe that all religions are valid paths to God, therefore there is no need to change to Christianity.
•Man is not a sinner in Hinduism. There is no need for a saviour.

Additional Difficulties in Accepting the Gospel
It is very difficult for a Hindu to accept salvation as a free gift without doing anything, for he grew up learning that salvation is to be earned by good works. He is supposed to live a good life by doing good. He can't understand why his good works do not count. Hindus believe in different things. They give importance to the faith of the believer, but not to the object of faith. They need to know that faith in things cannot save a person. The law of Karma makes it very difficult for a Hindu to accept forgiveness of sins. He does not understand why Jesus had to die for his sins. All these things need to be clarified and explained.

Points of Commonality and Contact
•Respect for scriptures. Hindus listen respectfully when you share from the Bible.
•Belief in incarnation. They need to be told that Jesus is the incarnation of God and His incarnation is unique, historical, and sufficient for all times.
•Belief in prayer and fasting. Stress the importance of these at times of special needs.
•Festivals, funerals, and weddings are special times. Invite

them to these occasions and they will get to hear the gospel.
•The person and the work of Christ. Hindus respect Jesus and appreciate His teachings. Focus on Jesus.
•The release from Karma. Hindus need to know about Jesus the Saviour and God's completed Karma on the cross.

Ways of Witnessing and Communicating the Gospel to a Hindu

How to Approach and Witness to a Hindu
•Establish friendship and meaningful relationships. Do not talk to a Hindu about religion in your first contact, unless he asks you a question. Build up your relationship and win his confidence and trust.
•Personal evangelism, one-on-one witnessing, and visiting. One-on-one witnessing is essential. Study their religion and have a good understanding of your religion as well. Naturally discuss spiritual matters. Find out what they know about Jesus and encourage them to study the Bible at least on an intellectual basis.

Asian Indians like their friends to visit them in their homes in times of joy, sorrow, and crisis. Use these times for witnessing. At first, do not visit too much. Never visit in a hurry. After your visit, leave something for them to read.

More Tips on Witnessing
•Accept him as he is, as a person created in the image of God. Speak in love.
•Sole authority of the Bible should be stressed. The most effective witness is consistent Christian living.
•Gospel must be presented to fit the values of his cultural background and his felt needs.
•Hindu society is community- and family-oriented and Guru-centered. Try to influence the whole family, particularly the head of the family.
•Help them understand that Christianity is not a western religion, but Christianity is Jesus Christ and very much oriental in its origin. He should be convinced that Christianity is socially and culturally acceptable.
•Help them understand that by receiving Christ, one does

not have to change one's own cultural and social patterns and political persuasions.

•Help them to understand that in Christ differences disappear. There is no east or west, high or low—all are equal.

•Help them understand that all religions are not the same and all do not teach the same things. Jesus is the only way to God.

•The Hindu mind is philosophical in nature, so use a philosophical approach with the educated people.

•Emphasize the uniqueness of Christ.

•Consistent prayer and faith in God and reliance upon the leadership of the Holy Spirit is important.

•Hindus living in the US are more open.

•Do not push, be patient, do not argue or insult, witness continually, and do not get frustrated with slow response.

•Quote the Scriptures, for the word of God is the power of God.

Other Methods and Approaches

Music and drama, scripture distribution, radio programs, cassette tapes, videotapes, films, Bible correspondence courses, and television programs are very effective means, especially in the language of the people.

◆

Meeting Muslims

Maurice Smith

The people who call themselves Muslims now represent one of the largest religious groups in the United States. Only a few years ago, Americans considered Islam (the religion of the Muslims) primarily the Arab way of life and a faith alien to the heritage of the United States. However, Muslims now live in many communities throughout the United States, not only practicing their faith but sharing it with others, including our friends, neighbors, and acquaintances.

Islam (literally submission) is the religion of people who claim to be totally submitted or dedicated to *Allah* (the Arabic term for "God"). The follower of Islam is a Muslim (or Moslem), "one who submits."

Nobody knows exactly how many Muslims live in the United States. Estimates of the number range from three to nine million; the most accurate assessment seems to be about five million. A steady stream of American converts to Islam has been joining a flow of immigrants to create a sizable Islamic community here. We can identify Muslims in the United States in five categories.

1. Visitors. Individuals holding visas and residing in the country temporarily include tourists, government representatives, business people, and students.

2. Immigrants. People from more than 60 countries also shape the Muslim community in the United States.

3. American converts. Conversion to Islam within America has not been restricted to people of African, Asian, and Middle Eastern heritage.

4. African-Americans who profess Islam. In the early 1930s, a black American, Elijah Muhammad, became the

leader of an anti-white, separatist organization called the Lost-Found Nation of Islam in the Wilderness of North America. Through the years the movement had at least five names. When Elijah Muhammad died in 1975, leadership passed to one of his sons, Warith Deen Muhammad. He changed the name and nature of the movement, intentionally moving it to be accepted as orthodox within the world community of Islam. In 1985 he officially disbanded the American Muslim Mission. The people now related to the movement are properly called simply, Muslims. It is incorrect to refer to them as Black Muslims.

5. Independent and quasi-Muslim groups. A schismatic group led by Louis Farrakhan has continued to espouse Elijah's original teachings and has maintained the name, Nation of Islam. Although it is not an authentic Islamic group, it claims to be, and many people confuse it with the larger, orthodox community associated with Warith D. Muhammad.

Background and Beliefs of Islam

Modern Islam began in the years between A.D. 610 and A.D. 632 in what is now Saudi Arabia. A man named Muhammad (also spelled Mohammed) said that God (Allah) spoke to him through the Angel Gabriel and dictated a series of messages that represented the will of God for all people. After Muhammad's death, these messages were collected into a book called the Qur'an (Koran)—"the recitation." Muslims do not call Muhammad the founder of Islam, for they consider Islam the world's original religion, believing that Adam, the ancient Hebrew prophets, and Jesus were "submitted ones."

Muslims deeply resent being called Mohammedans because they do not worship Muhammad, but consider him the seal of God's prophets. He brought the final revelation of God into the world. Jews and Christians are both People of the Book, but they failed to live up to the messages of the prophets and books God sent to them. For Muslims, the Qur'an, or Word of God, has the role that Christians give to Jesus Christ as the final Word of God.

Islam teaches that Jesus (Isa) was an important prophet

but not the Son of God. The Qur'an mentions Jesus ninety-seven times, giving Him titles greater than any figure before Him. He is called a sign and an example. He is called Messiah, Son of Mary, Messenger, Prophet, and Servant. Jesus is also called the Word of Allah. Muslims usually deny that Jesus died on the Cross, but say He ascended to paradise and He will return one day to complete His mission. In summary, Islam pictures Jesus as bringing the gospel as fulfillment of the Torah (Law), showing the signs of Allah, teaching prayer, and being a prophetic witness to the existence of Allah.

Muslims fulfill the fundamental duties of their faith by performing what they describe as the five pillars of Islam.

1. Shahada—the word of witness (recital of the creed), formulated in the statement: "I bear witness that there is no God but Allah, and Muhammad is the Messenger of Allah."

2. Salat—ritual prayer, required five times daily, either privately or in company with other Muslims.

3. Sawm—fasting during the daylight hours throughout the period of Ramadan (ninth month of the Islamic calendar).

4. Zakat—the giving of legal alms, a religious tax.

5. Hajj—the pilgrimage to Mecca, expected of every faithful Muslim at least once, with certain conditions.

How Muslims and Christians Perceive Each Other

Most Americans have no formal, accurate exposure to the history, teachings, and practice of Islam. At the same time, many immigrant Muslims have little knowledge of Americans, particularly Christian Americans. Christians and Muslims both tend to make broad generalizations about each other, unnecessarily fostering tensions. Many Christians do not know Muslims personally and have never visited in a Muslim home or had a Muslim family visit with them. Worship styles of Christians and Muslims are quite different. While people in both groups share many common terms, such as God, Jesus, prayer, sin, and devotion, they attach different meanings to those terms. We should not be surprised by these differences or let them hamper our attempts to meet Muslims cordially. Actually, talking about these differences graciously and amiably can open up opportunities for Christians and Muslims to know and understand each other better.

Meeting Muslims effectively and developing friendships with them is not always easy, but it is possible and appropriate for a Christian. Muslims are likely to be affected by cultural factors, a basic misunderstanding of Christianity, and a cautious resistance to Christianity, which they consider to be an inferior religion. Let this remind us of our critical need to be able to explain our own faith clearly, briefly, and in terms a Muslim can understand. And let us always be able to witness about our own understanding of Jesus with joy and assurance. Muslims do not have an assurance of going to heaven (for only Allah knows).

Witness to Muslims

Recognize that Islam teaches some ideas with which you as a Christian can agree. Whenever possible, let these ideas be points of contact that the Holy Spirit can use to bless your relationship with Muslims. Affirm to your Muslim neighbor how you believe that God (Allah) is One, God is Creator, God is sovereign, God reveals Himself and His will, and He wants us to respond to Him in faith and submission.

Recognize both similarities and differences between the Muslim and the Christian understandings of sin and salvation. Islam teaches that people are in a state of natural purity and always have a choice between good and evil. To Muslims, sin is the disobedience of responsible people to the law of Almighty God. Human weakness, forgetfulness, and a spirit of rebellion cause sin. Christians believe that people have chosen to sin against God, rejecting His nature and pursuing a course of life opposing God's essential character and revealed law. People need to be "saved," rescued from their persistent indifference and hostility toward God, and they are unable by their own efforts to achieve genuine righteousness and a right relationship with God.

Explain how Christians believe that God bestows His saving grace, not on the basis of one's faithfulness to perform religious rituals and to obey God's laws, but on the basis of one's repentance from sin and faith in the merit of Jesus. No one, not even the most devout believer, has the spiritual capacity to fulfill God's law completely. Ask your Muslim friends to consider the life and death of Jesus Christ as God's finest demonstration of His mercy and grace.

Deal graciously with Muslims' objections to, or misunderstandings of, Christian beliefs and practices (if Muslims bring up these issues). Explain that Christians are not guilty of shirk (the association of anything else with God). The Christian understanding of the Trinity does not mean that God is three gods, or that God is Father, Son, and Mary.

Introduce Muslims to the Bible appropriately, remembering that often they are unfamiliar with the Bible and have many misconceptions about it. Select a version that seems suitable for your Muslim friends, perhaps the Good News Bible. Explain the practical things about how to find the books, chapters, and verses. Ask them to let you read the Bible with them.

Remember that demonstrating by your own spirit and actions the character and message of Jesus surpasses argument, discussion, and even preaching. Be friends with Muslims without basing your friendship only on their willingness to become Christians. The distinguished missionary, Dwight L. Baker, observes that ministry is the most effective way to win Muslims to faith in Christ. "In my experience after 35 years of living and working among Muslims, I have never encountered a Muslim convert who said that he came to Christ as the result of some convincing arguments concerning the divinity of Christ. Nor have I heard any Christian worker make such a claim. . . . The conversion of a Muslim almost universally comes about through deeds of kindness and love."[1]

◆

Meeting People Involved in the New Age Movement

Maurice Smith

Trying to define the New Age movement resembles an effort to nail a bowl of gelatin to a post. The New Age movement is not a religion in the usual sense, though we can think of it as a religious system. It has no founder, no creed or statement of beliefs accepted by all the people involved in New Age, and no centralized leadership. Most people involved in New Age do not think of their involvement as an affiliation with a classical religion. Many New Age people also prefer to consider New Age as a spiritual system rather than as a religious system.[1]

Preliminary Questions

The first questions that arise as we meet people involved in the New Age movement are "What is the New Age movement?" and "How do I know when I have met somebody who is involved in it?" Traditionally, we meet people who identify themselves as belonging to, or in some way affiliated with, a specific religious group. Usually, we expect people to say that they are Buddhists, Hindus, Roman Catholics, Methodists, Southern Baptists, Jews, or something else familiar to us. However, when we meet people involved in the New Age movement, they may not even use the term New Age to describe themselves. Indeed, they may not even know that they are involved in something that can be considered New Age. Let us try to answer these first two questions before we consider other questions.

The term New Age movement is not an official name but an informal and imprecise label for a system of thought that encompasses a wide range of separate groups. We can refer to New Age as a movement in the same way as we refer to the sports movement, the health movement, or the civil rights movement. The New Age movement is really a series of movements; New Age people themselves refer to it as a network. The so-called New Age movement generally describes thousands of groups, organizations, teachers, techniques, products, writings, and programs that popularize Hindu and other Eastern-oriented religious concepts. New Age blends these concepts with American (and Western) interests in individualism, self-sufficiency, practicality, efficiency, and materialism. The New Age belief system is largely an Americanized variation of ideas inherent in Hinduism, Buddhism, and Taoism, ideas that have filtered into American life in the last 100 years.

Note these representative concepts that appeal to New Age-oriented people. (1) Reincarnation—the belief that a person goes through a series of lifetimes (incarnations). (2) A belief in the chakras, seven centers of supposed spiritual energy situated in the subtle body (which permeates the physical body)—an idea deriving directly from Hinduism. (3) A view of time as being a series of cycles rather than a linear process—a view in which there is no participation of a personal God having will and purpose. (4) Relativism—the view that all religious beliefs have value; religions represent different but valid paths to the same goal.

New Age is a way of thinking before anything else. It is a school of thought; it is a particular way of understanding reality. What we see as New Age beliefs, techniques, and activities develops out of the New Age view of the universe—the New Age world view. Elliot Miller, the Christian author of the book, *A Crash Course on the New Age Movement*, describes New Age as "an extremely large, loosely structured network of organizations and individuals bound together by common values . . . and a common vision (a coming 'new age' of peace and mass enlightenment)."[2] These common values or basic assumptions provide the core that enables New Age to hold together as a philosophical and religious system.

As a general rule, the following foundational ideas or presuppositions characterize a New Age movement, teacher, or activity: (1) All is one; all reality is a unitary whole; (2) Everything is God (god) and God (god) is everything; (3) You (as an individual) are God; you are one with all divinity; God is within you; (4) You will never die; you have lived before and you will live again (reincarnation); (5) Since the essence of reality is spirit or consciousness, you can create your own reality or transform your own consciousness; (6) There are no absolutes; individuals determine truth from their own intuition and experience; (7) Humanity's basic problem is ignorance, the loss of your awareness that you are one with everything; the solution to the basic human problem is enlightenment, the rediscovery of your true nature as divine; (8) A new world is coming; the world is on the verge of a New Age of enlightenment, love, and peace.

When you meet people who incorporate these assumptions into their thinking and into the ways they approach education, health care, ecology, economics, science, politics, religion, family, and personal decision making, you can be fairly sure that you have met "New Age people."

Subsequent Questions

When we meet people who embrace New Age ideas, at least two further questions arise: "Now, what do I say; and how do I explain my own faith in the most appropriate way?" Let us answer those questions by considering some guidelines for relating to people involved in New Age teaching.

1. Give careful thought to the way you phrase questions. Ask questions that are not offensive or condescending. Rather than stating, "Don't you believe in God?" inquire, "What is your understanding of God?" "Do you think of God as a Person of purpose and grace?" Instead of saying, "Do you believe in Jesus?" ask, "Where does Jesus Christ fit into all this?" or "What is your personal relationship to Jesus Christ?" Instead of asking questions like, "Do you believe in sin [or other subjects, such as justification or regeneration]?" phrase questions in terms that reflect the interests of New Age people. They respond better to statements like, "How do you explain the nature of humanity?"

and "Do you attach any meaning to personal faith in a transcendent, personal God?"

2. Inquire about people's understanding of the Bible. Recognize that they may not be acquainted with the Bible or may consider it irrelevant. New Age-oriented people often have a high regard for the Bible as sacred literature, but they rarely regard it as authoritative. Instead of asking, "Do you believe the Bible?" ask, "What is the role of the Bible for you?" Assume that New Age people may not be familiar with Bible books, characters, and episodes. References to David, the Apostle Paul, Luke, Hebrews, and the stoning of Stephen are likely to perplex New Age people. As you refer to, quote, or read specific Bible passages, let the Bible validate itself. The message of the Bible is true for your listeners, even when they do not consider it authoritative, because the Bible is authentically the Word of God. Invite people to read the Bible; give them one when you can. Explain such practical things as how to find the books, chapters, and verses. Suggest specific places to read. The marked New International Version New Testament, entitled *Born to Be Reborn*, is one of the best resources to give to people involved in New Age.

3. Talk about significant issues while keeping in mind the perspective and interests of New Age people. Plan your discussion along lines that fit the mindset in which New Agers are accustomed to thinking. You want to talk seriously about sin, salvation, the Christian life, and Jesus Christ—issues in which New Age people have very little interest. Therefore, get to those issues by tapping into the interests they do have. They think in terms of intuition and experience, enlightenment, personal transformation, and realizing their own divinity. Probe questions like the following:

• "How do you describe the basic human problem?" The typical New Age response will not refer to sin but to loss of people's awareness of their essential divinity. People in New Age profess that *the problem is outside*, in the ignorance, illusion, and evil in the world. For them, *the solution is inside*, in their own divinity. This gives you the opportunity to discuss the biblical understanding of the basic human problem—sin, humanity's estrangement from the holy, transcendent God. In the Christian view, *the problem is inside*, in a person's choice of a character that is opposed to the character of God, who is holy. *The solution is outside*, in the person and redemptive work of Jesus Christ, who reveals the transcendent God of grace. New Age appeals to people because the entire New Age system rejects the doctrine of sin. They do not seek forgiveness, but enlightenment. In such a setting you have the opportunity to talk about God, who is separate from humanity, but comes near and offers us a way to be restored to fellowship with Him.

• "What is your favorite way of seeking to change your life or being transformed?" An experience of transformation in one's life "is the common shared reality of New Agers."[3] Throughout the New Age community, there are hundreds of techniques that people employ to try to change their lives. New Age people call them "tools for transformation." Most New Age teachers, healers, lecturers, authors, counselors, and ministers want not only to teach ideas but to teach techniques or methods. As your New Age friends report this to you, you have an occasion to explain how Jesus Christ can change their lives, give them a new purpose, and *empower* them for living.

• "Tell me more about your perception of Jesus Christ." Remember that New Age disavows the uniqueness of Jesus Christ as fully God and fully human. In New Age, Christ is separate from Jesus, the way-shower. The "Christ" is the perfect God idea—the awareness of the divinity within. Jesus is not the only way to God; He is only one way among many. In such a discussion, you have a prime opportunity to say, "Let me tell you what Jesus Christ means to me."

4. Insist on defining terms, being aware that many words that both you and New Age people use have ambiguous meanings. Words such as love, spirit, peace, meditation, and wholeness, call for clarification. Most New Age people "believe in" God, Christ, transformation, life after death, and even heaven and hell; but what they mean by those concepts differs radically from the biblical ideas. As you meet people involved in New Age, be very careful that you understand what they are saying, and be sure that you help them understand what you mean.

◆

Meeting the Mormons

Tal Davis

I spoke to a couple in my home church who had visited Utah. They were impressed, to say the least, by the Church of Jesus Christ of Latter-day Saints (LDS or Mormons). "The highlight of our trip was our visit to Temple Square in Salt Lake City," they said. "It's the headquarters of the Mormon church. We heard the Mormon Tabernacle Choir perform, toured the various historical sites, and saw the presentations at the Visitors' Centers. We've never seen such strong devotion to God than in that place. We were especially struck by the many pictures and statues of Jesus and the testimonies of the young tour guides who showed us around. We had heard that Mormons weren't Christians, but they sure seemed like it to us. Why are other Christians so hesitant to accept them as fellow believers?"

It was a good question, and one that has been asked of me by Mormons themselves. It was obvious to the couple that Mormons present themselves as fine examples of Christian people. Most of us are aware of their clean living, wholesome life-styles, strong families, and patriotism. As Christians we commend them for those aspects of their religious devotion. Nonetheless, we must not be naive. Things are not always as they seem.

The LDS church has an effective public relations program that promotes their familiar positive image. That image, bolstered by the wholesome look of more than 45,000 LDS missionaries, has imbued itself in the American and world consciousness. As a result, the LDS church is having enormous success winning converts worldwide (about 300,000 a year) including many Christians who are drawn to their apparent devotion and life-styles. The LDS now claims 8 million members worldwide and 4.4 million in the US and Canada.[1]

What then is the truth about Mormonism? What do they believe? Is it an authentically Christian religion? Why would a Christian leave his or her church to become a Mormon? Can we, and should we, try to prevent it? These are important questions that Christians must answer since LDS churches are now located and growing, not just in Utah and the west, but in every state in the US, every province in Canada, and more than 120 countries worldwide.

LDS History: Prophets, Scriptures, and Persecutions

The Mormon movement began in the early 1800s with a New York farm boy named Joseph Smith, Jr. (1805-1844). Smith, according to his own story, as a teenager was confused as to which church he should join. He claimed that God the Father Himself and Jesus, His son, appeared to him in a wooded grove near his home, and told him he should join none of the churches because they were all in doctrinal error and spiritually corrupt.

Smith said that God provided for him the necessary ingredients to restore true Christianity to the earth, ingredients that had been lost for over 1500 years. Those ingredients included the office of Prophet, written scriptures besides the Bible, and two lost priesthoods without which true church authority could not function.[2]

The new scriptures included *The Book of Mormon*,[3] *The Doctrine and Covenants*,[4] and *The Pearl of Great Price*.[5] *The Book of Mormon*, according to Smith, was a collection of hidden books God allowed him to recover which described God's activity among several groups of Hebrews who had migrated to the American continents around 2300 B.C. and 600 B.C. The modern Native American populations were described as descendants of some of those immigrants. Today Mormons regard *The Book of Mormon* as a historically accurate account and place it even above the Bible as an inspired Scripture.[6]

The Doctrine and Covenants (D&C) is a collection of 138 supposed revelations and two declarations received by Joseph Smith and other LDS Presidents. These communications from God dealt with many theological and practical issues facing the early LDS movement, including some controversial topics such as the early practice of polygamy.[7]

The Pearl of Great Price is another collection of writings Joseph Smith claimed were of ancient divine origin.[8] This book, along with *The Doctrine and Covenants*, actually are more important as the sources of unusual LDS theology than are the Bible (the LDS recognizes the King James Version with some reservations) or *The Book of Mormon*.

Space will not allow me to describe the enormous problems the LDS faces for its claims of divine authorship of its extra-biblical scriptures. All lack even rudimentary archaeological and historical support. All have been altered many times by LDS editors without explanation. I recommend Harry L. Ropp's (with revisions by Wesley P. Walters) book *Are the Mormon Scriptures Reliable?* for a thorough evaluation of LDS scriptures.[9]

In 1844, it was revealed that the Mormons were secretly practicing polygamy. As a result, Joseph Smith, Jr. and his brother were murdered by an angry mob at a jail house in Carthage, Illinois. Brigham Young, one of Smith's right-hand men, succeeded him as President of the beset Mormons and led them west to avoid further persecution. In 1847 Young founded Salt Lake City, Utah and established there the permanent headquarters of the LDS church.

Years later, in 1890, under great political pressure, the LDS church officially ceased to sanction polygamy.

Today LDS members still regard their church as a uniquely ordained institution that alone bears the stamp of divine authority. They revere their current President, Ezra Taft Benson (1899-   ), as a living "Prophet, Seer, and Revelator" and their other "General Authorities" as the only divinely inspired proclaimers of God's word in the world today.[10] Thus, though they rarely state it bluntly anymore, Mormons regard all other Christian churches as spiritually inferior to their own.

LDS Beliefs
As remarkable as LDS history and church organization may be, that is only part of the story. Most Christians are only

45

familiar with the wholesome, Christian image Mormons present. Though we commend Mormons for many of their moral stances, we cannot honestly accept LDS doctrine as authentically Christian. There is not a single major doctrinal issue that Mormons and most Christians would agree on.

The most basic issue in any religious system is the doctrine of God. The historic Christian position, based on biblical teaching, is that there is only one eternally existent, all-powerful Creator God. Mormons, however, teach that the god of this world, who they refer to as "Heavenly Father," was once a man, like we are, who at one time lived on another world like this one. This god, who still exists with a physical body of flesh and bone, progressed in his spiritual development and obedience to *his* god and eventually became a god.[11] Heavenly Father and his wife procreated billions of spirit children in a preexistent spirit world. Thus, Mormons do not believe that God created the universe nor that He is uniquely divine. They teach that God only organized this world out of preexistent and eternal matter. Other gods rule other worlds.[12]

Mormons also believe that Jesus was one of Heavenly Father's children who also attained godhood. The Holy Ghost is another god. They teach that in his earthly life Jesus was the literal offspring of Heavenly Father and Mary. They say he died on the cross in order that we might be raised from the dead and have the opportunity to attain what they term exaltation.[13]

Exaltation is the uniquely Mormon view that human beings, if they are worthy and have accomplished everything necessary in this life, may progress to godhood. Therefore, the ultimate goal of all faithful Mormons is to become a god or goddess in the highest of three levels of eternal glory called the Celestial Kingdom. Mormons who attain that goal will repeat in another universe the same process Heavenly Father began in this universe.[14]

Mormons believe to attain godhood a number of requirements must be met. These requirements compose the LDS "Gospel" and include the following requisites.

The Mormon must have faith in God (Heavenly Father)

and worship him only. Mormons are warned against over-zealous worship of Jesus. A person must express sincere repentance, be baptized by immersion, and join the LDS church. The baptism must be performed by a LDS priest to be effectual. The Mormon must then have the laying on of hands for the receiving of the Holy Ghost.[15] All worthy male Mormons can receive the two LDS priesthoods. The lower priesthood is called the Aaronic Priesthood and the higher office is the Melchizedek Priesthood. All LDS leaders must have these two ordinations.[16]

Mormons who live righteous lives are expected to undertake what is called their temple work. LDS temples (44 worldwide) are edifices designed for conducting sacred rituals necessary for exaltation. Only Mormons who abide by the strict LDS code of conduct, called the Word of Wisdom, and live morally pure lives may even enter the sacred Houses of the Lord. The Word of Wisdom states that Mormons cannot drink alcohol, use tobacco, or indulge in "hot drinks" (ie. those with caffeine).[17]

Temple work consists of three ceremonies. First is the Mormon practice of baptism for the dead. Mormons believe that if someone died without having a chance to be baptized into the LDS church, someone else (usually a relative) can receive that ordinance on their behalf in the temple.[18]

The second ordinance is Celestial Marriage. This ceremony reflects the LDS belief that marriages and families are intended to last forever. Only husbands and wives who are sealed together in a temple will go on together to the Celestial Kingdom to become gods and goddesses.[19]

The third, and most closely guarded of the secret rituals, are the endowments. These ceremonies teach secret truths known only to Mormons about creation, the Fall, exaltation, etc.. Also, the Mormon is taught secret words, names, handshakes, and rituals believed necessary to get to the Celestial Kingdom.[20] The dead also can receive Celestial Marriages and endowments if faithful Mormons perform them on their behalf.

Mormons also are required to attend meetings of the local LDS congregations called wards. They are expected to participate in the weekly sacrament (Lord's Supper) meetings and contribute at least 10 percent of their income as a tithing.[21]

Most Christians, when first presented these facts about Mormon beliefs, are amazed. As my friends who visited Temple Square remarked, "They sure don't tell you all that when you take the tour!" Nonetheless, those doctrines are essential elements of LDS theology.

Mormons Winning Christians—Our Response

As stated previously, we respect and commend Mormons for the positive aspects of their faith. However, when we examine carefully the full scope of their beliefs in comparison to biblical Christianity we cannot consider Mormonism as authentically Christian. Mormon doctrines of God, Christ, salvation, and eternal life deviate drastically from historical Christianity.

This fact has important implications for Christians for two reasons. One is that many Christians, often unwittingly, have joined the LDS church. The other issue is that Mormons need to understand and worship the true God and Christ of the Bible.

Recently I read that a star college football player left his family's church and joined the LDS.[22] Occasionally I am asked, "Why would anyone leave their church to embrace such a radical faith as Mormonism?" The answer to that question is not simple. However, in most cases the reasons have little to do with theology. One researcher, Randal V. Outland, interviewed former Baptists who became Mormons. Outland found several factors that contributed to their becoming Mormons. The primary factor, he found, was social. Many had family or friends who were Mormons or they married a Mormon. This was apparently the football player's primary reason to convert; he was engaged to a Mormon girl at his college.[23]

Outland also found that the former Baptists were impressed by the dedication and commitment of their Mormon friends and missionaries. They had taken the missionaries' challenge to pray about the truth of *The Book of Mormon* and had become convinced.[24]

Many former Baptists felt that they did not get satisfactory answers to their doctrinal questions until they met the Mormons. They remarked that the churches they attended failed to teach and explain Baptist and Christian doctrine, especially the Trinity. Outland learned that many of them had experienced early Christian conversion. They were baptized as children but never adequately trained in Baptist doctrine or history.[25]

Outland concluded that churches must strive to retain members from becoming Mormons. He suggested that Christians must teach the Bible as the only authority for faith and practice, explaining clearly to new converts why it is true and reliable. He also argued that church leaders must teach biblical doctrines, especially those dealing with the nature of God, Christ, salvation, and eternal life.[26]

Christians also should be aware of the unconventional doctrines of the Mormon church and other sects and cults.

Perhaps the most important factor, according to Outland, is that people need to have a place where they are accepted and loved. If people do not find it in our churches, they are vulnerable prey for any new or unusual group that will promise it to them.[27]

Christians Winning Mormons—Our Responsibility
Christians must strive to prevent the loss of our people to Mormonism, but our responsibility does not stop there. We must also attempt, under God's direction, to win Mormons to a saving faith in Jesus Christ. That goal is not easy to accomplish even for the most experienced student of Mormonism and Christianity. To begin with, most Mormons assume they already have salvation because of their membership in the LDS church. Therefore, a Christian witness often must explain the critical differences between Mormonism and biblical Christianity. Also, the Mormon must be shown that salvation is based on faith alone in Jesus Christ as one's Saviour, and not church membership.

Christians should be familiar with biblical passages that contradict LDS doctrines to share with the Mormon. We must be careful, however, for the Mormon may quote Bible passages, often out of context, that he or she believes confirms LDS teachings. Also, we must establish clear definitions of all terms because Mormons and Christians use many of the same words but have completely different meanings. Most important is that we must take the time and effort to build personal relationships with Mormons. They rarely respond to the gospel in one encounter. Christians need to establish sincere friendships which include respectful discussions of faith.

◆

Meeting
Jehovah's Witnesses

Tal Davis

"Good morning," said a well-dressed young man who stood at my door. "We're in your neighborhood today talking to interested people about an article in this edition of *The Watchtower*.[1] The article is about how people can find security and peace in the midst of the problems of the world. Are you familiar with our materials?"

Of course, I immediately recognized the young man and his assistant as Jehovah's Witnesses (JWs), followers of an organization called The Watchtower Bible and Tract Society.

"I have some familiarity with your literature," I responded, "You're Jehovah's Witnesses aren't you?"

"That's right. Do you know about our organization?"

"I've studied about your beliefs and read some of your books. Come inside and let's talk about it."

I imagine most Christians have had encounters like the one above. Christians have been confronted by the zealous door-to-door proclaimers of Jehovah's Witnesses doctrine. Though most know Jehovah's Witnesses are unusual, and often are annoyed by their persistence, they do not understand much about their beliefs and practices.

That lack of understanding is unfortunate and even dangerous for two reasons. For one thing, it means that Christians may be vulnerable to attempts by JWs to confuse them about their own faith and proselyte them to the Jehovah's Witnesses movement. In my work at the Southern Baptist Convention's Home Mission Board's Interfaith Witness Department I often receive calls and letters from distraught parents, spouses, and pastors who share with me their concerns for a loved-one or parishioner who has begun studying with JWs. In some cases I have been able to warn the unwary person of the unbiblical nature of JWs teachings and prevent their further involvement. On other occasions, sadly, persons have gotten so deeply indoctrinated into JWs philosophy that I was unable to change their minds.

The second reason Christians need to know more about JWs is to be better equipped to share their faith in the true Jesus Christ with them. JWs need the assurance of eternal life that comes only by trusting in Jesus Christ as one's Saviour and Lord.

The Watchtower Bible and Tract Society today claims more than four million active members (called publishers) in 211 countries. In the United States and Canada more than a million people are engaged in JW activities. Perhaps the most remarkable fact about JWs is that in 1991 they reported more than 900 million hours of door-to-door visitation which resulted in more than 300,000 baptisms worldwide.[2]

The Jehovah's Witnesses thus pose a major challenge to Christian denominations as they spread their distorted gospel.

JWs History: Growth and Failed Prophecies
The Jehovah's Witnesses trace their beginnings to a disenchanted Pennsylvania Presbyterian named Charles Taze Russell (1852-1916). Russell, while still in his twenties, wrote several books predicting the date for Armageddon. He later began a magazine entitled *Zion's Watch Tower and Herald of Christ's Presence*, and gathered a group of followers into a Bible study. In 1884 he formally incorporated his movement as "Zion's Watchtower and Tract Society." Russell also wrote a series of seven books entitled *The Millennial Dawn*, in which he set forth his interpretations of biblical doctrines and outlined his theories about the coming end of the world. In 1909 he established his headquarters in Brooklyn, New York which he called Bethel. Today, Russell's organization has grown into one of the largest religious publication and distribution centers in the world now known as The Watchtower Bible and Tract Society (the Watchtower Society).[3]

Russell was followed as president of the Watchtower

Society by a flamboyant lawyer named Joseph Franklin Rutherford (1869-1942). Under his direction the movement continued to grow and adopted the name of Jehovah's Witnesses. Rutherford also wrote many books but was best known for his combative attitude toward other religions. He also made incorrect predictions for the last days that were quickly forgotten by his followers.[4] Nathan Knorr (1905-1977) took the reins next. Under his efficient leadership, the JWs grew from just more than 100,000 members in 1942 to more than 2 million worldwide in 1955.[5] The organization once again failed to date correctly the end of the world during his term, predicting that 1975 would be the date for Armageddon.[6] Today the JWs are led by 99 year-old Fredrick W. Franz (1893-   ). Franz, who joined the JWs in 1913 and for many years has been the preeminent theologian of the organization, continues to lead the JWs in the authoritarian process it has followed for over a century.[7]

Divine Authority by Committee

When the Jehovah's Witnesses come to your door they usually will insist that the Bible is their final authority for issues of doctrine and practice. The Watchword Bible and Tract Society claims to believe, with other evangelical Christians, that the 66 books of the Old Testament and New Testaments are the infallible Word of God.[8]

The problem with the JWs concept of biblical authority involves two factors. First, though they claim the Bible is inspired, they have produced a flawed translation that reflects their theological biases. The New World Translation of the Holy Scriptures (NWT) is the only translation the JWs acknowledge as accurate, yet it contains numerous revisions of passages found in standard translations. For example, John 1:1 of the NWT reads: "In [the] beginning the Word was, and the Word was with God, and the Word was *a god* (italics mine)."[9] That NWT translation differs significantly from all other versions. The New American Standard Bible (NASB) reads, "In the beginning was the Word, and the Word was with God, and the Word was God."[10] The NWT version of that verse reflects the Watchtower Bible and Tract

Society's biased opposition to the doctrine of the deity of Jesus Christ and is rejected by nearly every credible Greek scholar. Many other passages could be cited in the NWT that also reflect that same theological distortion.

The other problem JWs face, in regards to biblical authority, concerns interpretation. Often I ask JWs what books and Bible study aids they consult in coming to their doctrinal and practical conclusions. They inevitably show me copies of reference books such as *Aid to Bible Understanding* or *Reasoning from the Scriptures*.[11] They may also use Bible study guides like *You Can Live Forever in Paradise on Earth*.[12] In every case the study aids employed by JWs are only those published by The Watchtower Bible and Tract Society. Thus, the only sources of interpretation JWs utilize are those that reflect their own distorted views. In fact, JWs are prohibited from consulting scholarly commentaries and devotional helps not approved by their leaders.

What these facts mean, then, is that while JWs claim the Bible as their final authority, in reality, the leaders of The Watchtower Bible and Tract Society are the true decision makers for all issues of faith and practice. They claim to be God's *only* spirit-led organization in the world and all other churches are considered demonic. JWs are locked into the narrow, unscholarly doctrinal teachings of that organization with little input from outside sources.

As previously mentioned, the Watchtower Society is a religious conglomerate that publishes JWs materials and oversees a network of local congregations worldwide called Kingdom Halls. Though several thousand people work full-time for the organization, the true source of all authority rests in the president (Fredrick W. Franz) and a central committee called The Governing Body. These men are considered to be divinely inspired in their biblical research. However, an objective look at JWs history reveals many failed predictions for the end of the world, and numerous policies based on faulty biblical study (some of which they retracted).[13]

Jehovah is God (Jesus is a god)
When Jehovah's Witnesses visit homes initially they usually

do not discuss major points of doctrine. However, it does not take long to realize they have some very different ideas than do most Christians. Most evident is their references to God by the Old Testament term Jehovah. JWs do not believe in the historic Christian doctrine of the Trinity; rather they have a strictly unitarian concept of God as supreme creator-being of the universe.[14]

The most important implication of their doctrine of God is that they absolutely deny that Jesus Christ is God. Their contention is that Jesus ("the Word" in John 1) was Jehovah's first created being, through whom He then created the rest of the universe. They teach that he was Michael the Archangel in his preexistence, whose life-force was impregnated in the Virgin Mary. He lived a perfect life and did not sin, thus He alone was qualified to be the Messiah and pay the "ransom sacrifice" by His death to redeem mankind from sin. He was not crucified on a cross according to JWs, but was impaled on a torture stake. They also believe He was resurrected spiritually, not physically.[15]

Jehovah's Witnesses also deny both the personality and deity of the Holy Spirit. In the NWT "holy spirit" is never capitalized because they believe the holy spirit refers to the impersonal force of Jehovah, not to the third person of the Trinity.[16]

Salvation is Not Assured

Jehovah's Witnesses believe salvation comes through faith in Jehovah and active involvement in their organization. A person must be baptized into a JWs congregation, go door-to-door distributing literature and witnessing for Jehovah, and faithfully attend the Kingdom Hall.

The JWs believe in two types of salvation. The vast majority of JWs, called "other sheep," expect their salvation to consist of eternal life, not in heaven, but in a perfectly restored Paradise on earth. Only 144,000 JWs who are part of the Anointed Class and have exhibited the highest degrees of commitment will experience eternal life in heaven as co-rulers with the resurrected Jesus.[17]

Those who fail to obey the Watchtower Society's dictates can have no assurance of eternal life. Also, if one commits a heinous sin, publicly questions policies of the Watchtower Society, or associates with former Jehovah's Witnesses, he or she may be formally disfellowshipped from the organization. In that case, according to JWs belief, one has lost all hope of inheriting eternal life.

JWs thus have no concept of a present rebirth experience. They do not acknowledge that people can be sure of eternal life by grace through faith in Jesus Christ alone. Only those JWs safely within the Watchtower Society's protective canopy can hope for salvation.

Armageddon is Just Around the Corner

Jehovah's Witnesses, as previously indicated, have made numerous predictions concerning the date of Armageddon and the end of the world. Early in their history they pointed to the year 1914 as the inevitable time of the end. Based on faulty interpretations of the books of Daniel and Revelation and erroneous historical dating of several biblical events, the Watchtower Society concluded 1914 was the key year in Bible prophecy. When that date passed and the end did not occur, the Watchtower Society reinterpreted the date to be the end of the Gentile Times of 2520 years when Jesus secretly began the judgment of the world and Satan unleashed his fury against Jehovah's true servants (JWs).[18]

Sometime before this generation (those in the JWs in 1914) dies out, Armageddon will occur and Jehovah will pour out his judgment. According to JWs prophetic interpretations, only those who are faithful witnesses will be spared the destruction to come. Jesus will then rule from heaven for a thousand years, during which time people will be resurrected from the dead and given another opportunity to accept Jehovah's rule. At the end of the Millennium those who have been faithful will inherit Paradise on earth and the wicked will be annihilated from existence. JWs reject the doctrine of eternal hell for the lost.[19]

Opening the Door to Jehovah's Witnesses

When Jehovah's Witnesses used to come to my door, my inclination was curtly to tell them "No thank you" and close the door in their faces. Looking back, I think my attitude was based essentially on fear—I knew very little about JWs. I figured that as individuals they were somehow evil people. I now know that most JWs are normal people who have been deceived. I now believe it is incumbent on Christians to reach out, in love, to those locked in the Watchtower Society's bondage.

Over the years, I have learned several principles that may help accomplish this goal. These principles follow two areas of thought. One involves biblical interpretation and doctrine. The other involves our personal attitudes.

As Christians we must know what we believe and why we believe it. Churches need to follow sound principles of biblical interpretation and teach the historic doctrines of the Christian faith. Church leaders regularly should conduct studies that include the doctrines of God, the Trinity, the person and deity of Jesus Christ, the Holy Spirit, the way of salvation, the security of the believer, and views about the Second Coming. In addition, Christians need some introduction to the erroneous doctrines of the Jehovah's Witnesses and other cults.

The other side of the witnessing process involves how we relate to Jehovah's Witnesses. When they come to our door, or when we meet them in our daily lives, our attitude should be characterized by sincere love and service. We should treat them with respect and courtesy. Of course, we must decline to accept their teachings as authentically Christian and reject the claims of the Watchtower Society, but we must avoid unproductive arguments.

We should strive to establish personal relationships and show JWs we care about them as people while clearly presenting to them the biblical way of salvation. Witnessing to JWs requires nurturance and patience. Rarely is one led to Christ in the initial encounter.

◆

Meeting Members of The Way International

Tal Davis

Diane (not her real name) was a young woman from New York married to an Air Force officer stationed in the town where I was pastoring. Though not of our denomination, for several months she regularly attended our services. She enjoyed singing in the choir, and participated in some of the young women's functions. In an effort to discover her spiritual condition I asked her about her religious background. She indicated that she had not been raised in an evangelical church. She said that only a couple of years earlier she had begun to read the Bible and learn about Christ when she got involved in a nondenominational Bible study group.

Curious, I asked her what group sponsored the studies, expecting her to say Campus Crusade, the Navigators, InterVarsity, or some other Christian parachurch movement. "It was a group called The Way International," was her reply. "I was in a Bible study they call a Twig Fellowship. Have you heard of it? Incidently, my Twig Leader Sharon, from New York, is coming to visit me in a couple of weeks." At that time I had heard only a little about that organization, but what I had heard was not encouraging. I dug through books and files I had accumulated and found a booklet produced by the Interfaith Witness Department of the Home Mission Board of the Southern Baptist Convention which indicated that they considered The Way International to be an unbiblical cult.

Later I passed the booklet on to Diane and asked her to read it carefully and to give me her opinion. She never responded and not long after that I noticed she stopped attending our church. I learned that her Twig Leader indeed visited her from New York and apparently convinced Diane that she should not be associated with any other religious group except The Way International.

Since that sad encounter I have watched closely the activities of The Way International and researched its doctrines. What I learned was that The Way International is a large pseudo-christian cult that denies and radically redefines a number of essential doctrines of historic Christianity.

God Spoke Audibly to Founder

The Way International was founded by the late Victor Paul Wierwille, a former minister in the Evangelical and Reformed Church (now part of the United Church of Christ). The Way International's official biography of Wierwille states that, as a young man in the 1940s, he graduated from Mission House (Lakeland) College, studied at the University of Chicago, and earned a Master of Theology Degree from Princeton Theological Seminary. The organization's biographical statements also claim that he earned a Doctorate of Theology. The biographies, however, rarely indicate that the 1948 doctorate came from the now defunct Pike's Peak Seminary, an unaccredited school once located in Manitou Springs, Colorado.[1]

Wierwille claimed that, early in his ministry, he began to question some of the standard biblical interpretations of his and other Christian denominations. He stated that at one point he even took 3,000 theological books from his library, dropped them in a city dump, and determined to study the Bible alone.[2] Wierwille claimed that God Himself spoke to him audibly on October 3, 1942 and promised him that He would guide him accurately to understand, to interpret, and to teach the Bible (what Wierwille termed "working the Word").[3]

That date marked the beginning point for what in 1955 was incorporated as The Way, Inc. In the years following the initial calling Wierwille developed his program and organization. He established a headquarters on the site of his family farm in New Knoxville, Ohio. His Power for Abundant Living (PFAL) course was inaugurated in 1953 as the primary introduction to Wierwille's novel theology. The course, still taught by The Way International's staff, teaches

Wierwille's basic concepts about God, Christ, and specifically his notions about spiritual gifts and how to speak in tongues (a requirement for graduation).[4]

Wierwille's ministry grew slowly in the 1950s and early 1960s. However, it multiplied rapidly in the early 1970s on the coat-tails of the burgeoning Jesus movement and through Wierwilles' effective use of movies, cassettes, and video tapes. In 1971 he hosted his first Rock of Ages festival in New Knoxville for 1,000 people, a hundred of whom were commissioned as Word over the World (WOW) Ambassadors. That annual event reached an attendance of about 20,000 in the mid-1980s.

In 1975 Wierwille opened The Way College on the campus of what had been the College of Emporia in Emporia, Kansas. That same year, The Way, Inc. changed its name to The Way International and Wierwille issued the first edition of his most controversial book entitled *Jesus Christ is Not God*. Another ministry associated with the group which began in the 1970s was Outreach Athletes, a volunteer program geared toward professional athletes, teachers, medical workers, and the military. The Way International also sponsored TAKIT, a rock music band.[5]

In 1982 Wierwille, whose followers referred to affectionately as The Teacher, officially retired as president of The Way International and turned the organization's administrative leadership over to his then 33 year-old protege L. Craig Martindale. Martindale, who completed ten years as the group's president in 1992, is a former Southern Baptist who was active in the Baptist Student Union and the Fellowship of Christian Athletes while a student at the University of Kansas in the late 1960s. He joined The Way International in 1971 and worked his way up the leadership ladder.[6]

On May 20, 1985 Victor Paul Wierwille died at the age of 68 and was buried on the grounds of The Way International headquarters in New Knoxville. During his lifetime he managed to expand his organization to all 50 states and to as many as 45 foreign countries. Estimates put the total number of people who have been through a PFAL course to be as many as 300,000 worldwide.[7]

The Way Tree Grows

Under Wierwille's leadership, The Way International accomplished its plan using an efficient organization based on the metaphor of a tree. Individual members are called Leaves, who are banned together in small study cells called Twigs led by an elder or Twig Leader. A local association of Twigs is termed a Branch. A state organization of Branches is appropriately called a Limb. All the Limbs in a country are termed Trunks which are all tied to the world headquarters which is referred to as the Roots. This centralized and pyramidal scheme allows doctrinal statements, policy decisions, and discipline to flow smoothly from the top down (or in this case from the bottom roots up) to individual members. This process is characteristic of many authoritarian shepherding or discipling sects and cults.[8]

In the years since Wierwille's death The Way International has experienced some decline in membership. Annual attendance at the Rock of Ages festivals has dropped drastically in the last few years and in 1989 the organization closed The Way College in Kansas. Reasons for the drop may be attributed to several factors. For one, as is often the pattern when the charismatic leader/founder of a sect dies, the death of Victor Paul Wierwille left many of his followers without what they perceived as the divinely inspired leadership. Their loyalty was more to the man than to the organization. When he left the scene, these people were unimpressed by his successors in the group and left.

Another reason for the losses may be due to rumors that circulated shortly after Wierwille's death. He reportedly was accused of having committed adultery with several female members of The Way International over a long period of time.[9] He was also charged with plagiarism in some of his books.[10] These posthumously revealed flaws in The Teacher's character led to disillusionment with him and the organization by some adherents.

Another reason for The Way International's decline is due to several theological controversies that have arisen since Wierwille's death. These factors led to the establishment of several similar splinter groups led by former Wierwille followers.[11] I often wonder if Diane is still a part of this movement. My hope and prayer is that she has since discovered true faith in Christ.

Problems of Belief

My concern for her and others involved in The Way International runs deeper than just the nature of its organization. The Way International's major problem is its distorted version of biblical theology. Victor Paul Wierwille claimed he was more than just another teacher of the Bible, he claimed a special calling of God, in essence, to correct the erroneous interpretations and doctrines of Christianity.

Wierwille argued that the standard doctrines of most Christian denominations were based on faulty biblical texts and biased interpretations. He claimed that his studies had led him to conclude that nearly all standard Bible translations are flawed and lead to doctrinal errors. In fact, Wierwille's studies (which actually were based on the writings of several earlier so-called scholars) led him to discard some of the most important Christian doctrines and to adopt some bizarre notions.

For example, Wierwille argued that the New Testament should not include the four Gospels or the Book of Acts, but rather should begin with the Book of Romans.[12] Another novel belief he fostered was that Jesus was not crucified between two thieves, but rather nailed to a stake between four criminals (two on each side).[13] He also made a distinction between "Holy Spirit," which he saw as a synonym for God the Father, and "holy spirit," which he saw as an impersonal power given to believers from the Holy Spirit.[14]

Certainly Wierwille's greatest error centered on his ideas about the natures of God and Jesus Christ. He absolutely rejected the doctrine of the Trinity and denied the deity of Jesus Christ. Jesus, according to Wierwille, was born miraculously but did not have a preexistence. He argued that Jesus was nevertheless a perfect man whose soul was specially created by God and given the "holy spirit." Thus he can be called "the Son of God," but not "God the Son." Jesus then paid a legal transaction to redeem man from Satan by taking the sins of the world at his death and made "holy spirit" available to mankind by faith.[15]

Wierwille further said that a person receives a new birth upon a verbal confession of faith in Christ. However, one's mind is renewed to enjoy abundant life only by taking The Way International's PFAL class. The results of a renewed mind is that every believer is capable of manifesting all nine spiritual gifts of holy spirit (see 1 Cor. 12:7-10). Speaking in tongues specifically is the visible, outward proof of the invisible, inward experience of the holy spirit.[16]

Wierwille also taught the concept of conditional immortality or soul sleep. That doctrine, taught by a number of sects, states that at death one has no conscious existence until the resurrection at Christ's return. Thus he maintained that Jesus did not promise the repentant thief at his crucifixion that he would be with Him in Paradise *that* day, but a future time after His return.[17]

Can we reach those in The Way International?

I probably will never see Diane again. However, my experience and my research since then has led me to develop principles that I think an individual can follow to share a proper understanding of Christ with those who are still part of The Way International or who are considering joining it.

First, we need to be informed as to the doctrines and beliefs of our own faith. Perhaps one of the greatest weaknesses we have in our churches is a lack of knowledge about even basic Christian doctrinal concepts. A solid study of essential Christian theology is a must for any church. Pastors and church leaders should make sure new Christians are grounded in sound biblical doctrine.

Specific biblical study should focus on key doctrines such as the nature of God, the deity and work of Jesus Christ, the person and gifts of the Holy Spirit, the historic concept of the Trinity, the plan of salvation, and biblical teachings on life after death.

Second, we must be sure our motives are right. We must love unconditionally those in The Way International and communicate that fact to them. If I could talk to Diane I would let her know that my objections are not with her as a person, but with the faulty biblical interpretations of the organization. I would let her know that I respect her right to believe as she wills, but that I cannot in good conscience accept the teachings of Victor Paul Wierwille and The Way International as authentically Christian.

Third, I would engage Diane in a respectful exchange of beliefs and concepts. I would center the discussion, of course, on biblical concepts, emphasizing those passages concerning the deity and nature of Christ. I would make a list of specific passages and refer to them in the course of our conversation. I would express my own confidence of eternal life and abundant living through Christ and be ready to share clearly the plan of salvation.

Finally, I would encourage Diane to study the Bible for herself using materials and helps from sources other than those published by The Way International. I would seek to help her understand that the movement has no monopoly on interpreting the Bible. This may mean I might have to challenge her to investigate the claims of The Way International and Victor Paul Wierwille.

Many American young adults like Diane are being drawn into unorthodox religious movements. Christians must become better equipped to meet the growing challenge of cults both to prevent Christians from being deceived into joining these groups and to win those already involved in them to a saving knowledge of Jesus Christ.

Endnotes

Chapter 2. Meeting the Hispanic World

1. US Bureau of the Census, "Projections of the Hispanic Population: 1983-2080," Current Population Reports, Series P-25, no. 995, 1986.

2. Due to the limitations of space it will not be possible to focus on some of the smaller Hispanic groups, such as those who come from Spain, the Dominican Republic, etc.

3. US Bureau of the Census, "Hispanic Population in the United States: March, 1987" (Washington, DC: Government Printing Office, September 1987).

4. For more information about Mexican Americans see Carlos Cortés, "Mexicans," *Harvard Encyclopedia of Ethnic Groups* (Cambridge, MA: Belknap Press, 1980); James Diego Vigil, *From Indians to Chicanos* (London: C. V. Mosby Co, 1980); Virgilio Elizondo, *Galilean Journey: The Mexican American Promise* (Maryknoll, NY: Orbis Books, 1983).

5. Joseph Fitzpatrick, "Puerto Ricans," *Harvard Encyclopedia of Ethnic Groups*, (Cambridge, MA: Belknap Press, 1980), 858.

6. For additional information about Puerto Ricans, see Joseph P. Fitzpatrick, *Puerto Rican Americans: The Meaning of Migration to the Mainland* (Englewood Cliffs, NJ: Prentice-Hall, Inc.,1971); Francesco Cordasco and Eugene Bucchioni, eds., *The Puerto Rican Experience: A Sociological Sourcebook* (Totowa, N.J.: Ayer Co. Publ., 1973).

7. Lisandro Pérez, "Cubans," *Harvard Encyclopedia of Ethnic Groups* (Cambridge, MA: Belknap Press, 1980), 256-60.

8. This was due to a large extent to the fact that the Cuban government encouraged them to leave. To learn more about Cubans see Andrés Hernández, *The Cuban Minority in the US: Final Report on Need Identification and Program Evaluation* (Washington, DC, 1974); Eleanor Meyer Rogg, *The Assimilation of Cuban Exiles: The Role of Community and Class* (New York, 1974).

9. Ann Orlov and Reed Ueda, "Central and South Americans," *Harvard Encyclopedia of Ethnic Groups* (Cambridge, MA: Belknap Press, 1980), 210-16.

10. Ibid., 212.

11. Ibid., 216. For additional information about this group see Paul Cowen and Rachel Cowen, "For Hispanics It's Still the Promised Land," *New York Times Magazine*, 22 June, 1975; Karen DeWitt, "Washington's Hispanic Community Growing Rapidly," *New York Times Magazine*, 13 February, 1978.

12. Other factors which influence the rate and type of adaptation are patterns of residence (do they live in an isolated community?); length of residence (generally the longer they have been here the more extensive the adaptation); and attitudes

of the predominant society (is it receptive or resistent to the social assimilation of this group?).

13. Of the Cubans Americans, for instance, more than 51 percent of those 25 and over have completed high school and nearly 15 percent are college graduates. See *Harvard Encyclopedia* (Cambridge, MA: Belknap Press, 1980), 259.

14. Barbara Kantrowitz and Lourdes Rosado, "Falling Further Behind," *Newsweek*, 8 August, 1991, 60.

15. Vicky Larson, "The Flight of the Faithful," *Hispanic*, November 1990, 18-24.

Chapter 3. Meeting the Chinese World

1. Betty Lee Sung, *The Adjustment Experience of Chinese Immigrant Children in New York City* (New York: Center for Migration Studies, 1987), 228.

2. "Chinese in America," *The Ethnic Almanac*, 88; United States Department of Commerce, Census Bureau Press Release, 12 June, 1991, 2.; "The Economic Status of Americans of Asian Descent," *US Commission on Civil Rights, Draft Report*, July 1988, Table 8.1.

3. "Hong Kong, Countdown to 1997," *National Geographic*, February 1991, 124-25.

4. The Peters Projection map is available from Friendship Press, P. O. Box 37844, Cincinnati, OH 45222.

5. "Growing Up in White America, *Asian Week*, 25 May, 1990, 17.

6. Wing Y. So, "Identity and Identification," in *A Winning Combination: ABC, OBC*, Wally Yew, ed. (Petaluma, CA: Chinese Christian Mission, 1986), 31.

7. Bette Bao Lord, *Legacies: A Chinese Mosaic* (New York: Alfred A. Knopf, 1990), 5.

8. Sharon E. Mumper, "Repenting in Chine," *Evangelical Missions Quarterly* (July 1987), 314-30.

9. Winston Crawley, *Partners Across the Pacific* (Nashville: Broadman Press, 1986), 108-11.

Chapter 5. Meeting Muslims

1. *Understanding Islam: An Approach to Witness* (Waco, TX: Baptist Literacy Missions Center at Baylor, 1989), 102.

Chapter 6. Meeting People Involved in the New Age Movement

1. J. Gordon Melton, Jerome Clark, and Aidan A. Kelly, *New Age Encyclopedia* (Detroit: Gale Research Company, 1989), xiii.

2. Elliot Miller, *A Crash Course on the New Age Movement* (Grand Rapids, MI: Baker Book House, 1989), 15.

3. *New Age Encyclopedia*, xiii.

Chapter 7. Meeting the Mormons
1. *Church News* (Published by the Deseret News, Salt Lake City,UT), 5 October, 1991, 3.

2. Joseph Smith, Jr. *The Pearl of Great Price* (Salt Lake City, UT: The Church of Jesus Christ of Latter-day Saints, 1986), 47-59.

3. Joseph Smith, Jr. *The Book of Mormon-Another Testament of Jesus Christ* (Salt Lake City, UT: The Church of Jesus Christ of Latter-day Saints, 1986).

4. *The Doctrine and Covenants* (Salt Lake City, UT: The Church of Jesus Christ of Latter-day Saints, 1986).

5. *The Pearl of Great Price.*

6. Joseph Fielding Smith, comp. *Teachings of the Prophet Joseph Smith* (Salt Lake City, UT: Deseret Book Co., 1977), 194.

7. *The Doctrine and Covenants.*

8. *The Pearl of Great Price.*

9. Harry L. Ropp (with revisions by Wesley P. Walters) *Are the Mormon Scriptures Reliable?* (Downers Grove, IL: InterVarsity Press, 1987).

10. *Gospel Principles* (Salt Lake City, UT: Corporation of the President of The Church of Jesus Christ of Latter-day Saints, 1986), 43-46; 106-107.

11. Ibid, 5-6, 293.

12. Ibid, 9-12.

13. Ibid, 53-57; 65-71.

14. Ibid, 289-293.

15. Ibid, 110-134.

16. Ibid, 73-87.

17. Ibid, 181-182.

18. Ibid, 247-252.

19. *Achieving a Celestial Marriage-Student Manual* (Salt Lake City, UT: Corporation of the President of The Church of jesus Christ of Latter-day Saints, 1976), 130-132.

20. Bruce R. McConkie, *Mormon Doctrine* (Salt Lake City, UT: Bookcraft, 1979), 226-228.

21. *Gospel Principles*, 144-149; 197-200.

22. *USA Today*, 11 February, 1991, 2C.

23. Randal V. Outland, "Why Some Southern Baptists Become Mormons: A Project in Interfaith Understanding and Baptist Retention." (Dmin. diss., Southeastern Baptist Theological Seminary, 1989), 81.

24. Ibid, 82-88.

25. Ibid, 88-89.

26. Ibid, 90-100.

27. Ibid, 100-102.

Chapter 8. Meeting Jehovah's Witnesses

1. *The Watchtower* is published semi monthly by the Watchtower Bible and Tract Society of New York, Inc. 25 Columbia Heights, Brooklyn, NY 11201.

2. *The Watchtower*, 1 January, 1992, 10-13.

3. Anthony A. Hoekema, *Jehovah's Witnesses* (Grand Rapids, Mich.: Wm. B. Eerdmans Pub. Co., 1963), 9-14.

4. Ibid, 14-18.

5. *1977 Yearbook of Jehovah's Witnesses* (Brooklyn, NY: Watch Tower Bible and Tract Society of Pennsylvania, 1976), 31.

6. *The Watchtower*, 15 August, 1968, 494.

7. *The Watchtower*, 1 May, 1987, 22-30.

8. *Aid to Bible Understanding* (Brooklyn: Watch Tower Bible and Tract Society of Pennsylvania, 1971), 228-229.

9. *New World Translation of the Holy Scriptures* (Brooklyn: Watchtower Bible and Tract Society of New York, 1984), 1327.

10. *New American Standard Bible*, The Lockman Foundation, 1977.

11. *Reasoning from the Scriptures* (Brooklyn: Watch Tower Bible and Tract Society of Pennsylvania, 1985).

12. *You Can Live Forever in Paradise on Earth* (Brooklyn: Watch Tower Bible and Tract Society of Pennsylvania, 1982).

13. Raymond Franz, *Crisis of Conscience* (Atlanta: Commentary Press, 1983), 39f.

14. *Reasoning from the Scriptures*, 405-426.

15. *You Can Live Forever in Paradise on Earth*, 57f, 144.

16. *Reasoning from the Scriptures*, 380, 381.

17. *You Can Live Forever in Paradise on Earth*, 120-126.

18. Ibid, 141. See also: Carl Olof Jonsson, *The Gentile Times Reconsidered* (Atlanta: Commentary Press, 1983).

19. *You Can Live Forever in Paradise on Earth*, 81f.

Chapter 9. Meeting Members of The Way International

1. *The Teacher*, Dr. Victor Paul Wierwille (New Knoxville, OH: The Way International, 1985), 2-4.

2. John P. Juedes and Douglas V. Morton, *From "Vesper Chimes" to "The Way International" The Founder, History, and Activities of The Way Ministry* (Milwaukee: C.A.R.I.S., 1987) 11.

3. *The Teacher*, 4-5.

69

4. Leazer, Gary, *The Way International, An IWA Manual* (Atlanta: Home Mission Board, SBC, 1988), 2.

5. Juedes and Morton, 30.

6. "Profile: Rev. L. Craig Martindale" (The Way International, undated biographical sheet.)

7. *The Teacher*, 17.

8. Leazer, 21.

9. Keith Tolbert, "Infighting Trims Branches of The Way International," *Christianity Today*, Vol. 32, No. 3, 19 February, 1988, 44.

10. John P. Juedes and Jay Valusek, *Will The Real Author Please Stand Up?* (St. Louis: Personal Freedom Outreach, 1987), 14-15.

11. Tolbert, 44.

12. Victor Paul Wierwille, *Power for Abundant Living* (New Knoxville, OH: American Christian Press, 1971), 210-213.

13. Victor Paul Wierwille, *The Word's Way* (New Knoxville, OH: American Christian Press, 1972), 1-11.

14. Victor Paul Wierwille, *Receiving the Holy Spirit Today* (New Knoxville, OH: American Christian Press, 1971), 210-213.

15. Victor Paul Wierwille, *Jesus Christ is Not God* (New Knoxville, OH: American Christian Press, 1981).

16. Wierwille, *Receiving the Holy Spirit Today*, 41.

17. Victor Paul Wierwille, *Are the Dead Alive Now?* (New Knoxville, OH: American Christian Press, 1976), 77-83.

About the Writers

Mark Snowden is a consultant in the Global Media Resource Network at the Foreign Mission Board, Southern Baptist Convention.

Daniel Sanchez is an Associate Professor of Missions at Southwestern Baptist Theological Seminary.

C. Thomas Wright is Director, Materials Development, Evangelism Section at the Home Mission Board, Southern Baptist Convention.

Norma Charles is a home missionary in Atlanta, Georgia, where she seeks to reach the more than 10,000 Asian Indians in the area.

Maurice Smith serves as an Associate Director at the Interfaith Witness Department of the Home Mission Board, Southern Baptist Convention. He works primarily with world religions.

Tal Davis specializes in sectarian groups and new religious movements as an Associate Director at the Interfaith Witness Department of the Home Mission Board, Southern Baptist Convention.